CONNECTING CULTURES THROUGH FAMILY AND FOOD

The Mexican Family Table

By H.W. Poole

MASON CREST

Mason Crest
450 Parkway Drive, Suite D
Broomall, PA 19008
www.masoncrest.com

Printed and bound in the United States of America.

First printing
9 8 7 6 5 4 3 2 1

Series ISBN: 978-1-4222-4041-0
Hardback ISBN: 978-1-4222-4048-9
EBook ISBN: 978-1-4222-7746-1

Produced by Shoreline Publishing Group LLC
Santa Barbara, California
Editorial Director: James Buckley Jr.
Designer: Tom Carling
Production: Patty Kelley
www.shorelinepublishing.com
Front cover: Golden Pixels LLC/Alamy Stock Photo.

Library of Congress Cataloging-in-Publication Data
Names: Poole, Hilary W., author. Title: The Mexican family table / by H.W. Poole.
Description: Broomall, PA : Mason Crest, [2018] | Series: Connecting cultures through family and food | Includes
    bibliographical references and index.
Identifiers: LCCN 2017058183| ISBN 9781422240489 (hardback) | ISBN 9781422240410 (series) | ISBN
    9781422277461 (ebook)
Subjects: LCSH: Mexican American cooking--Juvenile literature. | Mexican Americans--Food--Juvenile literature. |
    Food habits--Mexico--Juvenile literature. | Mexico--Social life and customs--Juvenile literature. | United States--
    Emigration and immigration--Juvenile literature.
Classification: LCC TX716.M4 P656 2018 | DDC 641.59/26872073--dc23 LC record available at https://lccn.loc.
    gov/2017058183

QR Codes disclaimer:

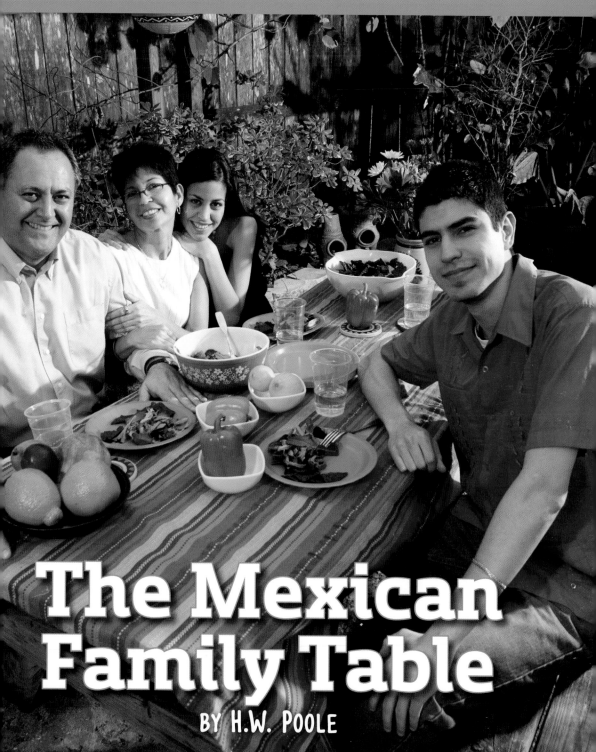

The Mexican Family Table

BY H.W. POOLE

Contents

KEY ICONS TO LOOK FOR

 Words to Understand: These words with their easy-to-understand definitions will increase the reader's understanding of the text, while building vocabulary skills.

 Sidebars: This boxed material within the main text allows readers to build knowledge, gain insights, explore possibilities, and broaden their perspectives by weaving together additional information to provide realistic and holistic perspectives.

 Educational Videos: Readers can view videos by scanning our QR codes, providing them with additional educational content to supplement the text. Examples include news coverage, moments in history, speeches, iconic moments, and much more!

 Text-Dependent Questions: These questions send the reader back to the text for more careful attention to the evidence presented here.

 Research Projects: Readers are pointed toward areas of further inquiry connected to each chapter. Suggestions are provided for projects that encourage deeper research and analysis.

 Series Glossary of Key Terms: This back-of-the-book glossary contains terminology used throughout this series. Words found here increase the reader's ability to read and comprehend higher-level books and articles in this field.

Introduction

Ask an average American to describe Mexican food, and you're likely to hear about hamburger meat stuffed in hard-shell tacos or tortilla chips topped with a bright yellow, cheese-like substance. But what passes for Mexican at fast-food restaurants in the United States bears no resemblance to the true cuisine of Mexico.

Anglo America has always had a complicated relationship with its southern neighbor. Perhaps that's because, as recently as 200 years ago, much of what we now call America was in fact Mexico: The states of Alta California, Nuevo Mexico, and Coahuila y Texas were part of Mexico until the mid-18th century. The Treaty of Guadalupe Hidalgo in 1846 not only brought an end to the Mexican-American War, but also completely reshaped the political geography of North America. Thousands of people went to bed one night as Mexicans and woke up the next morning as Americans.

This matters because when we talk about contemporary Mexicans emigrating to the United States, it's important to remember how much of their heritage is already here. You can see it not only in the state names of California, New Mexico, and Texas, but also in the names of streets, towns, churches, and schools all over the Southwest. You can also see it in the ethnic heritage, customs, and foods of the people who live there. As Mexican Americans sometimes point out, "We didn't cross the border; the border crossed us."

Mexican culture has been woven into the American fabric from the beginning. And in many western states these days, the population of people with Hispanic heritage matches or even outpaces the population of people without. Too often, we use the pronoun "they" to mark people as outsiders. But Mexican Americans are not "they" at all. *They* are us.

As for the cuisine of Mexico, it's the result of hundreds of years of cultural mixing—from ancient cultures like the Maya and the Aztec to the Spanish conquistadors of the 16th century, and from the Caribbean influence in the south to the arrival of French and Italian cuisine from Europe. The complex flavors and preparations of authentic Mexican food are popular with American "foodies"; in fact, trend-spotters regularly announce that "upscale" Mexican food is about to become the next big thing in fine dining. But while we await the coming "authentic Mexican" food revolution, these days hard-shell tacos and chips with salsa reign supreme in American supermarkets. The fact is, tacos and nachos are as American as apple pie.

Getting Here

It's the dead of night in Jacumba Desert. Desperate people fleeing Mexico and points farther south have entrusted their lives to the *coyotajes* (**coyotes**). Risking death from heat exposure, dehydration, or venomous bites from snakes and scorpions, they cross a no-man's land between Mexico and the United States in search of a better life in the north.

All of us have heard this story. Perhaps we've seen it in films or on TV, or maybe we even know someone who made the journey. It's a **stereotype** of illegal border

Words to Understand

coyotes   people who help sneak others into the United States for a fee

exploitation   treating someone unfairly while benefiting from that person's labor

reunification   bringing people who've been separated back together

stereotype   an oversimplified assumption about a person or group

turbulence   here, describes a situation that is uncertain and can change rapidly

Not every person from Mexico emigrates to the United States through the desert, but for those who do, it can be a difficult and dangerous journey.

crossings, but it certainly does happen. However, you might be surprised to hear that it happens much less often these days than it once did.

Sneaking over the border is not the only way people from Mexico immigrate to America—far from it. For example, between 4,000 and 5,000 TN-2 visas are issued annually. The TN-2 program, part of the North American Free Trade Agreement (NAFTA), provides for legal, job-related immigration from Mexico to the States. But about 95 percent of legal immigration from Mexico is due to the family **reunification** program, which provides legal status to close family members of Mexicans who are already in America.

The reality of Mexican immigration is far too complex to be captured by sound bites, slogans, or stereotypes. To understand it better, and to understand the many ways that Mexican immigrants have influenced our country and culture, it's important to first understand some history.

The Bracero Program

The rough outline of the US-Mexican border was established in 1848, when Mexico lost about half its land area to America under the Treaty of Guadalupe Hidalgo. After the treaty, only a tiny number of Mexicans immigrated to the United States. In fact, people were more likely to travel in the other direction—Mexicans who chose not to suddenly become Americans traveled southward to be reunited with their families. It wasn't until the early 20th century that Mexicans began heading north in large numbers.

Two main factors inspired these moves. One was economic—both the industrial and agricultural sectors of the US economy expanded rapidly, providing opportunities for laborers who were willing to work hard in

Thousands of men from Mexico took advantage of the Bracero program to move to the United States for good-paying, if hard, work.

factories or fields. The second factor was the Mexican Revolution, which began in 1910. Although the revolution officially ended in 1920, **turbulence** from it continued for years afterward. The violence and economic uncertainty in Mexico forced many thousands of people from their homes. In the 1920s, the United States was taking in as many as 100,000 Mexicans per year.

It might sound strange, given the 21st century politics surrounding immigration, but in the 1920s, Mexicans were usually accepted by native-born Americans. At the time, America was also seeing a lot of immigration from southern Europe and Asia—and it was those immigrants who were viewed with suspicion. That's not to say that Mexicans did not experience discrimination, because they definitely did. But in comparison to other newcomers, Mexicans were considered to be good workers and important contributors to the US economy. For example, the Immigration Act of 1924 ended immigration from most of the world, but not from Mexico. Powerful forces in the agriculture industry wanted to make sure that Mexican labor was still available.

The Great Depression of the 1930s caused the US economy to shrink, resulting in widespread unemployment among native-born Americans and immigrants alike. As so often happens when the economy sours, people turned on the most vulnerable newcomers, blaming them for the economic crisis. Racism against Mexican immigrants increased noticeably. In the

Men in the Bracero program showed off their support of the United States at this train station rally.

early 1930s, federal and state governments began undertaking something called repatriation, which is a nice-sounding word for deportation.

"It was announced," wrote historian Francisco Balderrama, "that we need to provide jobs for Americans, and so we need to get rid of these other people. [Officials told people that] you would be better off in Mexico, here are your train tickets. You should be ready to go." Repatriation programs forced more than a million people out of the country, and not just Mexican citizens. In fact, about 60 percent of those sent "back home" were American citizens who happened to be ethnically Mexican.

Despite this, Mexican immigration spiked again just a few years later. As World War II ramped up, politicians changed their minds about Mexican labor. They worried that the war effort would result in mass labor shortages, and these fears led to the creation of the Mexican Farm Labor Program. Informally known as the Bracero program (*bracero* is a Spanish word for farm laborer), this legislation brought millions of Mexicans

1962 film on Bracero program

into the United States as guest workers, and many stayed. Thirty states participated in the Bracero program, but by far the largest number of workers went to California, Arizona, and Texas.

The Mexican government hailed the program as "a noble adventure for our youth," but in truth it tended to be the poorest and most vulnerable workers who became braceros. The vast majority were employed in the agricultural sector, but not all: During World War II, about 100,000

Americanization Through Homemaking

In the early 20th century, Mexicans were widely considered to be "good" immigrants as opposed to what many people thought of as "bad" immigrants flooding in from southern Europe. But although Mexican immigrants may have been preferred over certain other groups, that's not to say that Mexican culture was respected. Programs sprang up across the Southwest to try and "Americanize" newcomers as quickly as possible. Food and diet were considered to be a

Americanization Through Homemaking

BY

PEARL IDELIA ELLIS
Department of Americanization and Homemaking,
Covina City Elementary Schools

WETZEL PUBLISHING CO., INC.
336 SOUTH BROADWAY
LOS ANGELES, CALIF.
1929

key component of this undertaking. To these "do-gooders," creating good Americans meant eliminating as much Mexican food from their diets as possible.

For example, in a 1929 pamphlet called "Americanization Through Homemaking," author Pearl Idelia Ellis lists the types of foods she thinks Mexican immigrants *should* be eating, including peanut butter soup, boiled spinach, and orange sherbet. She also asserts, incorrectly, that eating tortillas at lunch makes students "lazy" and prone to "take food from the lunch boxes of more fortunate children."

This auto crossing between Tijuana, Mexico, and San Diego, California, can often be among the most crowded and busiest in the world.

Mexican guest workers were employed by the railroads. Despite regulations designed to protect them, the workers often worked long hours in terrible conditions for little pay.

Modern Immigration

Although the Bracero program was inspired by wartime labor shortages, it stayed in place long past the end of the war. It was finally shut down in 1965, in hopes of ending the **exploitation** of low-wage guest workers. But the reality is that the jobs—on farms, construction sites, and elsewhere—still needed to be filled. Meanwhile, young men who couldn't find work in Mexico were still eager to do those jobs. And if there was no legal way in? People found other ways.

Well-intentioned as it may have been, the end of the Bracero program was also the beginning of mass illegal immigration. According to Douglas Massey of Princeton University, by 1979 the United States was receiving roughly the same number of Mexican immigrants as it had been in the 1950s, but the vast majority were undocumented (that is, did not have legal immigration papers). The same pattern that developed in the early 20th century has continued. In times of political and economic instability in Mexico, emigration to the United States increases; when times are tough in America, the travel flows in the other direction.

For instance, in the mid-1990s, Mexico (and in fact, much of Central and South America) experienced severe economic problems, and this

Many people make the crossing between Mexico and the United States every day, heading to and from work or school.

resulted in larger numbers of people coming to the United States to seek employment. But when the United States faced its own economic crisis in 2007 and 2008, larger numbers of Mexicans returned south to find work.

And now? Surveys suggest that about two-thirds of Americans believe illegal border crossings are increasing. The exact opposite is true. The Department of Homeland Security estimates that in 2005 roughly 1.5 million people crossed into the United States from the south. Ten years later, stricter enforcement had gotten that number down to 170,000 people.

The *Financial Times* reported in 2017 that Mexican immigration was at a 48-year low. The rate of Mexico-to-United States immigration is "net negative," meaning that more Mexicans leave the United States than arrive. This is partly due to stricter enforcement: About 3 million undocumented Mexican immigrants were deported during the Barack Obama administration (2008–2016). A still-difficult job market in the United States is another factor causing people to return to Mexico.

Text-Dependent Questions:

1. Roughly how many TN-2 visas are issued to Mexican citizens annually?

2. What is "Americanization"?

3. How many people entered the United States illegally via the southern border in 2005? How many did so in 2015?

Research Project:

Find out more about the Bracero program. What was life like for the workers? What arguments were made for and against the program? How are these arguments similar to or different from current immigration debates?

SNACKS AND STREET FOOD

When you hear the words "Mexican food" and "snacks," visions of nachos may not be far behind. And while there's nothing wrong with a big plate of cheesy chips, Mexican cuisine has a lot more to offer when it comes to snacks and quick bites purchased from vendors. All the cities in Mexico—and the capital of Mexico City most especially—enjoy a thriving street food culture. More and more, these dishes are making their way to parts of the United States that are home to people of Mexican descent.

Tamales
These wrapped delights are a signature dish of Mexican cuisine. Shredded meat—often but not always pork—is cooked with chilis and spread on masa (a dough made from corn flour), then wrapped in a corn husk and steamed. In the United States, tamales are strongly associated with Christmas (see page 48), but they are a common street food in Mexico, where they are purchased from tamal carts.

Elotes
A popular street food throughout Mexico, elotes are also popular among Mexican Americans and can be prepared fairly easily at home. Grilled corn on the cob is topped with a mix of crema (Mexican sour cream) or mayonnaise, cheese, lime juice, chili powder, and salt. A related dish is esquites, in which the corn is removed from the cob and served in a bowl with the same toppings.

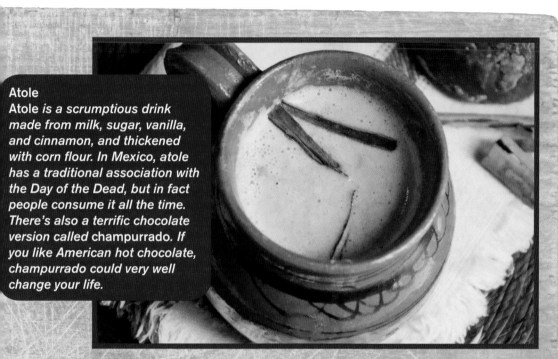

Atole
Atole *is a scrumptious drink made from milk, sugar, vanilla, and cinnamon, and thickened with corn flour. In Mexico, atole has a traditional association with the Day of the Dead, but in fact people consume it all the time. There's also a terrific chocolate version called* champurrado. *If you like American hot chocolate, champurrado could very well change your life.*

Chicharrones
This is the Mexican version of what Southerners might recognize as cracklings—bits of pork belly fried with the skin still on. Chicharrones are especially popular with kids, who get them from vendors after school.

SNACKS AND STREET FOOD

Gorditas

The word gordita *is Spanish for "chubby one," and these corn tortilla pockets stuffed with meat and cheese definitely live up to the name. There are many regional variations in how gorditas are made—some are large while some are bite-size, some are fried while some are baked. Depending where you are, gorditas might include tomatoes, guacamole, potatoes, beans, eggs, sausage, or other ingredients. Just know this: A true gordita has nothing in common with the Taco Bell version, which is basically just a flatbread taco.*

Churros

Fried sticks of pastry sprinkled with cinnamon and sugar or dipped in chocolate, churros are a staple of street fairs all over the United States. But in their home country of Mexico, churros are considered a breakfast food, to be enjoyed with a cup of cafe con leche (coffee with milk).

Salsa Verde
Salsa verde can be found in nearly every Mexican home. It's used to add extra heat to practically any dish you can think of.

Ingredients:
  1 lb tomatillos
  2 serrano chiles, seeds removed and chopped
  1/2 cup cilantro, chopped
  2 T onion, chopped
  Salt

Preparation:
1. Prepare the tomatillos by removing the outer husks and washing thoroughly.
2. Simmer the tomatillos in water for about 10 minutes, until they are soft. Drain them, but save some of the cooking water for the next step.
3. Put the tomatillos, the rest of the ingredients, and about 1/2 cup of cooking water into a blender. The mixture should be fairly liquid but with some chunks left in it. (Add more water if needed.)
4. Add salt to your taste and serve with tortilla chips or tacos or anything you like!

Settling In

In the 1920s, a woman named Aurora Guerrero was living in the village of Huanusco, in the southwest part of Mexico. She was raising three young children on her own; like so many others, her husband had traveled north in search of farm work in the United States. Eventually, Guerrero had had enough. She packed up the children and headed for California in search of her husband.

She didn't find him, but she did find tremendous success with the restaurant she founded in 1934: Cielito Lindo, on Olvera Street in downtown Los Angeles. Initially, Cielito Lindo only had a few wooden tables. They didn't even have running water at first—they had to get it from a nearby gas station! But Angelenos couldn't get enough of Guerrero's taquitos, which are small corn tortilla tacos

Words to Understand

feminization a process in which something becomes more associated with women

munitions military weaponry

wholesale a business that sells goods to other businesses for resale

Olvera Street in downtown Los Angeles has been preserved as a reminder of early Mexican influence on the area; it has become a popular tourist spot.

that are rolled, fried, and slathered in avocado sauce.

In San Diego around the same time, tortilla factory owner Ralph Pesqueria was asked to create a portable lunch for the employees of Consolidated Aircraft, a **munitions** plant just across the street. Independently of Guerrero, he, too, began selling a small fried taco—Pesqueria claims he is the one who thought of the name "taquito"—that was a huge hit with customers. So much so that Pesqueria opened the El Indio Mexican Restaurant in 1940.

Regardless of who invented them, taquitos are unquestionably an American creation. In Mexico, small fried tacos are called *flautas*. Unlike taquitos, they are made with flour tortillas, not corn, and they are served with toppings like cabbage or queso fresco (a type of cheese).

Flautas are a popular Mexican meal, here with avocado sauce.

Working with Food

Guerrero's life story represents a typical (if highly successful) path for Mexican immigrants. It's important to note that there is no single immigrant experience—every person's life and history are unique in some way. But a substantial percentage of Mexicans who emigrate to the United States find employment in some aspect of the food business. From growing the food to preparing it, serving it, and cleaning up afterward, many recent immigrants begin their new lives in food-related jobs.

There's no doubt that fruit and vegetable farms would have a tough time surviving without Mexican and Mexican American labor. By one estimate, 95 percent of California farm workers are of Mexican background.

In addition to growing food, another common job for recent Mexican immigrants involves preparing it. And the work isn't limited to Mexican

Keeping It In the Family

Both Cielito Lindo and El Indio are still going strong all these years later. And as of 2017, both restaurants were being run by family members. Guerrero's granddaughter, Susanna, runs Cielito Lindo, while El Indio is run by Pesqueria's son, Ralph Pesqueria, Jr., and his granddaughter.

restaurants—Mexican immigrants work in all kinds of professional kitchens. As chef and TV host Anthony Bourdain notes, "I worked in French and Italian restaurants my whole career. But really, if I think about it, they were Mexican restaurants and Ecuadorian restaurants, because the majority of the cooks and the people working with me were from those countries. That's who... showed me what to do when I walked in and didn't know anything."

Enrique Garcia Salazar moved to Minneapolis from a tiny village called Quebrantadero. When he arrived, he had a contact in the restaurant business, because he'd worked at a bakery back in Mexico. Unfortunately, he didn't actually know how to cook, so he started off washing dishes. But Salazar set his sights on learning the trade. "After that," he told an interviewer, "I cooked French food, Italian food, and American food." But his wife's family had once sold tamales for a living back in Mexico, and so when he got the opportunity, Salazar opened a restaurant using his

Guy Fieri in a Mexican restaurant

mother-in-law's recipes. La Loma Tamales started in an 80-square-foot space in South Minneapolis; by 2017 he had expanded to several more locations and added a **wholesale** business.

Family Life

L.A.'s Aurora Guerrero was a trailblazer in another sense. Historically, immigration from Mexico involved men heading north to work and sending money back to their families. But that began to change in the late 20th century, in a phenomenon that sociologists call "the **feminization** of migration." Increasingly, it's women following Guerrero's footsteps, heading north to find work in the United States. According to the

In neighborhoods with a large Mexican immigrant population, the shops, such as this butcher's, cater to their traditional needs.

US Census Bureau, there were about 1.9 million female Mexican immigrants in 1980; that number had grown to 5.6 million by 2014.

Regardless of whether it's the father or the mother who migrates north for work, temporary family separations are fairly common for Mexican immigrants. Sometimes families separate on purpose, when a parent emigrates in search of work. But sometimes the separation is forced, due to deportation. This is a constant worry for many, because it's not uncommon for Mexican American families to have both documented and undocumented members. This is referred to as "mixed immigration status." A 2016 study from the Migration Policy Institute reported that 5.1 million children have at least one parent who is undocumented. That's 7 percent of all American kids, though of course not all are Mexican Americans.

Recent US government policy changes have created worry and protests in the Mexican American community, among many others.

For example, a man named Armando López entered the United States illegally and lived in Nevada for 27 years. Despite his undocumented status, he ran a business and paid taxes, married, and had five children. But he was deported in 2016 due to a traffic violation. His wife, Ana, who is also undocumented, and his children, who are US citizens, stayed behind.

Ana has lived in the United States since she was 15 years old. She feels that she's living in limbo; she lives in fear that she, too, will be deported. But at the same time, she has lived in the United States for so long that she has no connection to Mexico. "I'm not from here," she told a *Financial Times* reporter in 2017, "and I'm not from there." She asked the reporter to change her name in the article, because she feared being separated from her children.

Text-Dependent Questions:

1. Who were Aurora Guerrero and Ralph Pesqueria, Sr.?

2. What percentage of farm workers in California are of Mexican background?

3. About how many children in the United States have a parent who is undocumented?

Research Project:

Some people say the United States should be a "melting pot," while others say it should be more like a "salad bowl." Research these concepts to find out what they mean, and decide which description you think is more accurate and/or desirable. Write a short essay defending your choice.

SOUPS AND SALAD

It's common for Mexican meals to begin with soup, and soups and stews are also frequently sold by street vendors. A number of soups are also strongly associated with holiday meals, as you'll see.

Sopa Azteca
A tomato-based chicken and chile soup, served with tortilla chips, cheese, and avocado. The soup is popular all across Mexico, but there are numerous regional variations in how it's prepared. In Michoacán, a state in the southern part of the country where the soup originated, ancho chiles are usually used.

Birria
This slow-cooked goat stew was born in Guadalajara, in the state of Jalisco. The goat is marinated in adobo spices, steamed, and roasted before being served as stew. The entire goat goes in this dish—even the head, horns and all!

Menudo
This traditional Mexican soup is made with beef stomach, also known as tripe. The tripe is cooked in a broth with chile peppers, onions, garlic, cilantro, lime, and other ingredients. In the United States, menudo is often eaten as a first course, while in Mexico it's more likely to be served as a part of family celebrations such as weddings or during the Christmas holidays.

Posole
Another dish that's closely associated with Christmas in Mexico, posole is either a thin stew or a hearty soup, depending on your point of view. Posole is Spanish for "hominy," a form of dried corn that is also the main ingredient in the dish.

Connecting

Nathanel Valera was born to Mexican immigrants who were living and working in St. Paul, Minnesota. Shortly before his second birthday, his father was deported; to keep the family together, his mother brought Nathanel back to Mexico City to live. But she'd often remind her son that he was a US citizen, explaining that someday he'd return to the United States. That day came when Nathanel was a teenager—he went to live with his uncle in St. Paul, to attend school and work part time. Meanwhile, his parents and younger brother remain in Mexico.

Words to Understand

assimilate here, to integrate or blend in

iconic considered to be a perfect symbol or representation of a broader idea

incentive motivation

proximity nearness in space or time

quantify to measure something in numbers

variant a variation of something

Children born of immigrant parents in the United States are automatically US citizens, which has created consequences for the status of the parents.

The specifics of Nathanel's story are uniquely his, but the split family situation is a fairly common one for many Mexican immigrants. When people immigrate to the United States from, say, China or Nigeria, they usually do so with the expectation that they won't return to their birth country very often, if at all. But geography creates a somewhat different situation for many Mexican immigrants—the **proximity** of the two countries leads to stronger ties with their home country. This is sometimes called living *"de aquí y allá,"* or "here and there," with connections to people on both sides of the border.

Chili or Chile?

Is *chili* a meal or a fruit? What about *chile*? It depends who you ask. A dictionary will probably tell you that the words are interchangeable, but there are a lot of people who would strongly disagree!

In Nahuatl, the language of the Aztecs, the word for hot peppers is *chilli*. The word was picked up by the Spanish, while in English the **variant** spellings of *chili* and *chile* emerged. Over time, chili came to refer to the Texas state dish of beef, onions, and spices. *Chile*, on the other hand, refers to the family of peppers that give so many Mexican foods their heat.

Becoming American?

No matter where they're from, all immigrants eventually face the question of just how "American" they want to become. There are lots of factors influencing that decision—and often it isn't even a conscious choice. Even if an immigrant doesn't try hard to **assimilate**, he or she is likely to gradually start picking up American ways, and the following generation absolutely will become more assimilated than their parents.

For Mexican immigrants living "*de aquí y allá*," the assimilation process may be slower than is typical. After all, if half your family remains

American consumers have made Mexican food one of the most popular ethnic foods in the country, with a wide variety of casual and family restaurants.

in Mexico, or if you are unsure about how long you'll even stay in the United States, you may be less inclined to transform yourself. If you live in constant fear of being deported, it's understandable that you would not feel there is much **incentive** to assimilate.

The Manhattan Institute issues a regular report based on something called the Assimilation Index, which attempts to **quantify** levels of assimilation based on things like labor force participation, ability to speak English, intermarriage, military service, and much more. They found that immigrants from Mexico do take longer to assimilate than, for instance, Vietnamese immigrants, who tend to assimilate the quickest. Also, the closer people live to the border, the lower their assimilation rate tends to

In places such as El Paso, Texas, the Mexican American community shares traditions such as dancing with their neighbors.

be: For instance, assimilation among immigrants in Toledo, Ohio, is quite high, while in Waco, Texas, the rate is lower.

Unfortunately, the American media don't always give an accurate impression of immigration reality. For instance, surveys have shown that the majority of Americans believe that at least two-thirds of all immigrants are undocumented, but that's untrue. The truth is that it's less than a third of immigrants who are illegal. In fact, Mexican immigrants are the largest group of legal, green card holders in the United States. In 2017 there were about 11.9 million green card holders, 37 percent of whom were born in Mexico.

Unfortunately, while most Mexicans report that they want to become US citizens, they become citizens at noticeably lower rates than people of other nationalities. According to the US Census Bureau, 67 percent of immigrants who were eligible to apply for citizenship had done so by 2015. But among Mexicans, only 42 percent had applied for and received citizenship by that date. In most cases, this was not due to lack of interest: The people surveyed reported that cost and the language barrier were the main reasons why they did not apply.

That's Mexican Food? Really?

An irony of Mexican American life is that, while their culture (and their food especially) is embraced by non-Mexicans, the actual Mexican immigrants living among us are frequently disrespected. Consider the contrast of President Donald Trump: On the one hand, he kicked off his 2016 presidential campaign with a speech declaring that most Mexican immigrants are criminals; on the other, he marked Cinco de Mayo that year by posing for a photograph where he grinned over a bowl of taco salad.

Of course, there's nothing very Mexican about taco salad in the first place. It was invented in the 1950s by Texas-based businessman Elmer Doolin, who also founded the Fritos corn chip empire. Doolin piled meat, cheese, and other ingredients on top of a pile of his Fritos and the taco salad was born. It was first introduced to the public at Disneyland, where Doolin was an early investor, at his theme restaurant, Casa de Fritos.

The invention of the taco salad is a fairly typical story in the history of Mexican food in the United States—or perhaps we should say, Mexican-ish food. A Mexican citizen who just arrived in the United States wouldn't recognize many of the foods that Anglos think of as "typical Mexican foods."

Traditional tacos are made in soft tortillas such as these, not the hard, crunchy type developed for the American market.

For example, the taco is an **iconic** food item on both sides of the border, but it's not really the same dish in the north as it is the south. In Mexico, a taco is a freshly made corn tortilla—not fried (think soft American tacos)—that is wrapped around a meat filling (but steak, sausage, or pork, not ground hamburger). Traditional Mexican tacos may have cilantro and onions as toppings but they don't usually have lettuce or tomatoes. (The salad is eaten on the side, not on the taco.) And traditional Mexican tacos don't have cheese—a taco with cheese would be a quesadilla, not a taco.

In fact, many of the so-called Mexican dishes you might know from the local fast-food place are actually American inventions. The burrito as you probably know it—a giant flour tortilla overstuffed with beans,

 ## Run for the Border

Those hard-shell tacos you've come to expect at the school lunch counter were invented because the fresh tortillas of authentic Mexican tacos are not "shelf-stable," meaning they don't last for very long. If the tortillas are fried, they keep longer, and if they are fried in a U shape, they are both easy to stack and present an obvious holder for the rest of the food.

The fried taco shell was popularized (although not invented) by a businessman named Glen Bell. Bell wanted to apply the fast-food principles that were so successful at McDonald's to Mexican food, and it certainly worked. The restaurant he created, Taco Bell, has more than 6,000 franchises across 22 countries.

rice, cheese, meat, and maybe the occasional vegetable—is a variation of the Mexican dish called *tacos de harina*, a more modest food in which one or two ingredients are wrapped in a (smaller) flour tortilla. People in the northern part of Mexico do eat burritos, but most Mexicans would consider them to be "tourist food," not real Mexican food. (The origins of the burrito as you know it are not entirely clear, but it may have been created to feed soldiers on the move during the Mexican American War.)

Nachos were invented by Ignacia "Nacho" Anaya at a restaurant called the Victory Club in 1943. Anaya was trying to please a group of American women whose husbands were soldiers stationed at Fort Duncan, in Texas. He threw together some ingredients he found lying around in the kitchen—tortillas, cheese, and jalapeños—and named the dish after himself: Nacho's especial.

People who consider themselves foodies may scoff at American-style tacos, burritos, and nachos. But the fact that these popular dishes are not

Interview with taco history author

authentic Mexican dishes does not necessarily make them fake or bad. It just makes them more American than Mexican.

Seeking (and Finding) Success

If you ask recent immigrants about what motivated them to come to the United States, one answer you'll hear quite often is, "I want my children to have a better life." So it seems fair to ask: Does that happen? Do the children of immigrants succeed in achieving what their parents hoped for?

A 2014 study by sociologists Jennifer Lee and Min Zhou looked at this question by investigating the educational achievements of the children of immigrants in Los Angeles. They studied families from China, Vietnam,

The popular party food nachos got its name from the Mexican inventor.

Many American-born children of Mexican immigrants become the first people in their families to attend college.

and Mexico. Children of Chinese immigrants achieved the highest levels of education overall, but they also started off with the most educated parents.

Mexican immigrants, on the other hand, tended to come from less well-off, less educated backgrounds. When it comes to improving on the achievements of their parents—that is, getting that better life that their parents dream of—Mexican American kids are actually the most successful of all the groups in the study. Children of Mexican immigrants graduate from high school at twice the rate their parents did, and they graduate from college at twice the rate of their fathers and three times the rate of their mothers.

Meanwhile, in 2013, the rate of college enrollment among high school graduates of Hispanic background hit 49 percent, surpassing the rate among non-Hispanic high school graduates, which is 47 percent. Contrary to racist stereotypes, the majority of Mexican immigrants come here to work and they come here to learn—and we can see the results in the educational successes of their young people.

Text-Dependent Questions:

1. What does the phrase "*de aquí y allá*," mean? What phenomenon does it describe?

2. What's the most important spice in Yucatan dishes?

3. Who invented nachos and why?

Research Project:

Go online and find a menu for a Mexican fast-food restaurant like Taco Bell or Chipotle. Choose a dish that interests you and find out what that dish is like in the Mexican style as opposed to the fast-food style. What has been altered about the dish? Why do you think those changes were made?

Great Variety

The Cuisines of Mexico

Mexican cuisine varies a great deal, depending on what part of the country you are in. Here are just a few of the key regions (there are others!) and their unique approaches to food.

Yucatan Peninsula

At the far south end of the country, the Yucatan separates the Caribbean from the Gulf of Mexico, and for a long time it was fairly isolated from the rest of the country. The cuisine is strongly influenced by the Mayans, the people who dominated the area for thousands of years. Yucatan dishes use a lot of tropical fruits such as limes, tamarind, and bitter orange. The most popular chile pepper in this region is the habañero, which is small but packs in a lot of heat! The key spice in Yucatan cooking is *achiote*; it gives dishes a yellowish color.

Oaxaca

The mountains and valleys in the southern state of Oaxaca once served as obstacles to Spanish settlers. As a result, the region's cuisine has retained a stronger-than-usual indigenous influence, from the ancient cultures of the Zapotecs and their conquerers, the Mixtecs. In particular, the region is famous for its various kinds of mole (moh-LAY) sauce; in fact, Oaxaca is sometimes referred to as "the land of the seven moles." Mole sauces are made with various combinations of chile peppers and, famously, some are made with chocolate—although they are not chocolate tasting.

Central Mexico

The dishes produced in and around Mexico City are often what most people think of when they think of Mexican food. This is where you'll find street food like tacos, tortas, and chalupas. Beef or lamb that's slow-cooked over an open flame is called *barbacoa*, and it's another **iconic** component of this region's cuisine.

Northern Mexico

Cattle ranchers have long dominated the arid north, which means that beef often dominates the plates. This is also the area where flour tortillas—so popular in America, but so strange to most Mexicans—are consumed regularly. *Norteño* (northern) restaurants are the place to go for a burrito, and you may also recognize their refried pinto beans, as those are now a staple of Mexican restaurants all over the United States.

MAIN COURSE

If you've ever been to a Mexican restaurant, you're probably familiar with the combination plate. You can choose a couple of items—maybe a taco and an enchilada, or a burrito and chile poblano—and it comes to you with rice and beans on the side. The combination plate was invented by Mexican-American restaurants in Texas in the early 1900s, to please Anglo customers who expected large, sit-down meals. (These same restaurants also pioneered selling combination plates by number, rather than name—it was a way for English speakers to order without having to try to pronounce the Spanish names of the dishes.)

In Mexico itself, people are far more likely to eat a meal that starts with soup or rice and is followed by a main course, with warm tortillas served on the side.

Picadillo
In the United States, this is often called Mexican Picadillo, simply because other Latin cultures have their own versions. Picadillo is ground beef that's cooked with chiles, spices, and vegetables (and sometimes with raisins for sweetness). It can be eaten with rice or used as a filling for tacos or empanadas. There is also a delicious Oaxacan version made with pork instead of beef.

Chiles en Nogada

Green chiles are stuffed with meat and cheese, topped with a cream-based sauce and some pomegranate seeds. Because its colors are green, red, and white, chiles en nogada is a popular dish for Mexican Independence Day (September 15).

Mole Poblano

Mole is a popular type of sauce that comes in a variety of different preparations. The most famous by far is mole poblano—in fact, it is sometimes called the national dish of Mexico. If made in the traditional way, the labor-intensive dish has 30 or more ingredients, but lots of shortcuts have been designed over the years. The full ingredient list includes five different chile peppers, cinnamon sticks, peanuts, pumpkin and coriander seeds, and Mexican chocolate. The sauce is most commonly served on turkey or chicken, but it can be used on other meats, as well.

Reaching Back

For some Americans, the Christmas season means shopping trips to the mall, hanging a wreath on the front door, or putting up the Christmas tree. But for many people of Mexican heritage, Christmas hasn't truly arrived until there's been a *tamalada*.

A *tamalada* is a gathering of family and friends—often presided over by someone's *abuela* (grandmother)—who work together to create tamales for Christmas. Tamales are delicious but **labor-intensive**, so the best way to do it is to gather a big group to make a large number of them. Tamaladas usually feature an assembly line, in which each person has a particular job: preparing the *masa* (corn flour dough), spreading it to the correct thickness, adding ingredients, tying the tamale

Words to Understand

labor-intensive   describes something that takes a lot of work to create

procession   here, a parade

remittance   payment

Tamales are a popular Mexican dish at Christmas time. Here, the chef has made a masa *from black beans and is putting it into tamale wrappings.*

in its corn husk wrapping, and so on. Some tamaladas gather together more than just one family—they can involve a whole community making literally thousands of tamales all at once.

Churches in Mexican American communities often host tamaladas, and not just at Christmas. For example, the New Life Baptist Church in Knoxville, Tennessee, funds its mission projects through its Famous Hot Tamale sales. Meanwhile, at the Apostolic Church of Indio, near Palm Springs, California, Becky Montes is in charge of the tamale assembly line. "There's a camaraderie that's involved when you're making tamales," she told a reporter in 2016. "It's hard for just one person to make them, but if you have your sisters, your aunties, your grandmother come over to help, it's just a special thing."

Las Posadas

For Mexican Americans, there's much more to Christmas than just the tamales. Las Posadas has been a Christmas tradition in Mexico for hundreds of years, and the tradition has been transmitted to the United States, albeit with some adjustments. In Spanish, *las posadas* means "lodging"; the holiday celebration reenacts the long search of Mary and Joseph for a room at an inn. Traditionally, Las Posadas lasts for nine days, to mark the nine months of Mary's pregnancy. Celebrants walk in a **procession**, with one person playing Mary, one Joseph, and the rest following. They knock on doors, sing songs, and ask to be allowed to enter. The "innkeeper" (or host) lets them in for prayers and food. Typical dishes include tamales, glazed ham, and a spicy soup called menudo.

Out of a desire to become more American, it used to be common for Mexican immigrants to shrink Las Posadas down to just one night rather than nine, or even skip it entirely. But the practice of celebrating a full Las Posadas has made a comeback in recent years. Of course, there are sometimes adjustments made: For example, people celebrating Las Posadas in northern states sometimes hold the entire procession indoors, due to un-Mexico-like winter weather.

Cinco de Mayo

Christmas time provides a lot of opportunities for Mexican Americans to connect with their culture, but that's far from the only time. For example, the spring holiday of Cinco de Mayo (May 5th) is an important celebration, and it's enjoyed by plenty of Anglos as well.

Mexican Americans and many other Latino Catholics take part in the Las Posadas parades during Christmas time.

You might have heard that Cinco de Mayo is Mexican independence day, but that's incorrect; the country's actual independence day is celebrated in September. Cinco de Mayo marks the Battle of Puebla in 1862, in which a Mexican army of about 2,000 men defeated an invading French force that was about three times the size. A remarkable battle, to be sure, but Cinco de Mayo is not an especially important holiday in Mexico itself. (Mother's Day, which is celebrated around the same time, is far more important in Mexico.)

In the United States, an interesting thing occurred. The Battle of Puebla took place around the same time the US Civil War began. The Union army, which was not that successful in the early battles of the war, took inspiration to keep going from the success of the Mexican fighters.

Local Mexican-Americans take part in a Cinco de Mayo parade in Denver, Colorado, one of many celebrations held across America.

It's important to remember that France was supporting the Confederate side at the time. In fact, Napoleon III's plan was to conquer Mexico and turn it into a pro-Confederate French colony. Consequently, the soldiers of Puebla who defeated the French were viewed as brothers in arms by the Union. Cinco de Mayo was embraced by Mexican Americans as a way to celebrate their ethnicity *and* demonstrate their patriotism at the same time. In the words of historian Jose Alamillo, "They were able to link the struggle of Mexico to the struggle of the Civil War."

As the years passed, Mexican Americans began paying increasing amounts of attention to Cinco de Mayo—throwing parades, banquets, and even bull fights. The Chicano rights movement of the 1950s and 1960s, also known as *El Movimento*, inspired an expansion of Cinco de Mayo activities, as more and more people of Mexican ethnicity wanted to celebrate their heritage. But even so, observance of the holiday was largely limited to immigrant communities... until the liquor companies got involved.

The San Antonio-based importers of the beers Corona and Casa Modelo funded the first Cinco de Mayo-based marketing campaign in 1989. The success of that campaign led them to repeat and expand it the following year. Ever since, Cinco de Mayo has been promoted all across the United States, to people of every ethnicity. These days, more than $600 million worth of beer is sold every Cinco de Mayo—that's even more than on St. Patrick's Day, another celebration that strives to connect cultural pride with alcohol sales.

Cinco de Mayo is a bit like St. Patrick's Day, actually. Just as everybody is Irish on St. Pat's, so everyone is Mexican on Cinco de Mayo. Consider the many Irish bars that serve tacos stuffed with corned beef and dress their wait staff in shirts saying, "Irish I was Mexican." As Alamillo put it, "[Cinco de Mayo is] not a Mexican holiday, not an American holiday, but an American-Mexican holiday."

Day of the Dead

In the fall, Mexicans and many Mexican Americans celebrate a two-day holiday known as *Dia de los Muertos* (Day of the Dead). The tradition is more than 500 years old; it evolved as a blend of the Catholic holidays of All Souls Day and All Saints Day, along with the traditions of the indigenous peoples of Mexico. The idea is that at midnight on November 1, the gates of heaven are opened and the spirits of children are able to reunite with their loved ones; then, the following day, the spirits of adults are present on Earth. Dia de los Muertos not only honors those who've died

Colorful painted skulls are among the traditional decorations and art created for and around the Dia de los Muertos *events.*

Dia De Los Muertos, or the Day of the Dead, is an annual three-day celebration that honors the dead

Day of the Dead celebrations

but also reminds the living that we will all pass eventually. In the words of artist and political commentator Jose Guadalupe Posada, "*Todos somos calaveras*" ("We are all skeletons").

Ofrendas (altars or offerings) are made in homes, graves are cleaned in cemeteries, and there are parades in the street. In 2017, a four-mile parade through the streets of Mexico City was enjoyed by some 300,000 people.

Food is a huge part of Dia de los Muertos celebrations. There's a special kind of sweet bread, *pan de muerto*, that's made just for the occasion. The traditional drinks of Dia de los Muertos celebrations are *atole* (see page 19) and a fermented agave beverage called *pulque*. Food is also placed on the altars as offerings to the dead after their long journey from the other world.

Mexican Americans celebrate Dia de los Muertos in much the same way. Like Cinco de Mayo, the November celebrations were popularized in the United States as part of the Chicano civil rights movement. Today, major cities in the United States enjoy massive celebrations. For instance, in Los Angeles, public celebrations of Dia de los Muertos began in 1972 and have occurred annually ever since: Some 15,000 Angelenos take part in activities organized by the Chicano art collective known as Self Help Graphics & Art. Other big cities, such as New York, Houston, Chicago, Phoenix, and Seattle, all have various kinds of Dia de los Muertos celebrations, including festivals, parades, and concerts.

Remittances

Holidays like Dia de los Muertos and Cinco de Mayo provide ways for immigrants to connect with their cultural heritage in a general sense. But immigrants from Mexico also stay in touch via far more direct routes. In fact, many families in Mexico depend on their Mexican American relatives for financial support.

The money immigrants send back home is called **remittances**, and Mexican Americans are major contributors. About 40 percent of all remittances sent out of the United States go to Mexico: In the single month of March 2017, Mexican Americans sent a record-breaking $2.5 billion back to Mexico. Annually, remittances to Mexico are roughly $24 billion—that's more income for Mexico than the country receives from its petroleum exports.

Remittances have been rising every year since 2014, and analysts are not entirely sure why. Part of the reason may be that Mexican immigrants are staying longer in the United States than they used to. The median length of stay has jumped from seven years to 12—possibly because stronger enforcement of immigration laws makes it riskier for Mexicans to go back and forth. Interestingly, remittances have continued to go up even as the actual number of Mexicans coming to the United States has gone down.

Many people in Mexico depend on these funds from relatives and friends in the United States. The average amount sent is around $300, about 14 times per year. The amount jumps up in times of crisis, such as the weeks and months immediately following Mexico's devastating earthquake in September 2017.

Chicano Culture

The Civil Rights Movement that began when Rosa Parks refused to give up her seat on a bus in Alabama in 1955 was an inspiration to people across the country, and Mexican Americans were no exception. Their own civil rights movement, *El Movimiento*, began in the late 1960s. Leaders such as Reies López Tijerina in New Mexico, Cesar Chavez and

This march was one of many in the late 1960s for Chicano rights.

Dolores Huerta in California, and La Raza Unida party in Texas inspired Mexican Americans to organize on behalf of workers' rights, improved education, voting rights, and other economic and social issues.

Alongside the fight for civil rights, a cultural movement was born, with writers, musicians, and artists seeking to define an identity that was neither American nor Mexican but both at once—a uniquely Chicano identity. Rodolfo "Corky" Gonzalez may have written the first clear explanation of Chicano identity with his stirring 1967 poem, "Yo soy Joaquin" ("I am Joaquin").

The development of a hybrid Mexican American identity has also influenced the world of food. Los Angeles-based chef Wes Avila described the fusion of Mexican and American cuisine as "Alta California"—a nod to the original name of the state, back when it was part of Mexico. Chefs are blending the traditions of "la cocina de la abuela" (grandma's kitchen) with the techniques of high-end restaurants to create a whole new type of food. Alta California cuisine might mean tacos stuffed with uni or squid, for instance, or French fries topped with mole sauce.

Alta California cuisine is an example of what sociologists call "selective accultura-

Cesar Chavez remains a hero to many for his work on behalf of migrant workers.

tion," which refers to immigrants taking on some aspects of a new culture while also retaining connections to their birth culture. Being fluent in both English and Spanish is one example of selective acculturation: The person doesn't toss out her old language, but instead she adds another skill to use in her new surroundings. While old-fashioned assimilation ("becoming Americanized") can be seen as a process of subtraction—get rid of that old language, get rid of those old customs—selective acculturation is a process of addition. As journalist Sarah Menkedick wrote in her analysis of Mexican American culture, "The goal isn't for Mexican culture to become a colorful sequence of parades and piñatas adorning the…Anglo mainstream, but rather to be a reservoir of deeper meaning for immigrants, offering them a foothold of purpose, history, and connection."

Text-Dependent Questions:

1. What is a *tamalada*?

2. What did Jose Guadalupe Posada mean when he wrote, "*Todos somos calaveras*"?

3. What is the average size of a remittance sent from America to Mexico? How often is that money sent?

Research Project:

Find out more about the history of *El Movimiento*. What concerns sparked the movement? Who were its leaders? What impact did the movement have on the United States generally?

DESSERT

After a meal that is often filled with spice, Mexican restaurants offer a variety of softer, sweeter foods. As with many parts of their foodways, Mexican chefs call on traditions from within and from outside their land to wrap up their meals with a sugary touch.

Flan
Every Mexican restaurant serves flan, but in fact this custard dates back to ancient Rome; that's why so many European countries have some sort of flan-like dessert in their repertoire. Spanish invaders brought the flan recipe with them to their colonial outposts, and Mexican cooks have been creating all kinds of varieties ever since—coffee, chocolate, and pumpkin, among many others.

Pastel de tres leches
As the name suggests, this cake is made with three dairy products—condensed milk, evaporated milk, and heavy cream. A sponge cake is soaked in the milks to create the creamy texture. And in case that's not enough dairy in one bite, it's served with whipped cream on top.

Dulce de leche
Made by slow-cooking milk and sugar, dulce de leche is popular all over Mexico and, indeed, throughout Central and Latin America, as well. There are many variations on the dish, such as cajeta, *which is made from goat's milk, and* manjar blanco, *which is vanilla flavored.*

Arroz con leche
Otherwise known as rice pudding, arroz con leche is another Spanish import to Mexico. Rice is cooked with some water and cinnamon, then evaporated and condensed milk are added, creating a sweet, lumpy pudding.

Find Out More

Books and Articles

Arellano, Gustavo. *Taco USA: How Mexican Food Conquered America.* New York: Scribner, 2012.

Green Card Youth Voices: Immigration Stories from a St. Paul High School. Minneapolis, MN: Wise Ink Creative Publishing, 2017.

Menkedick, Sarah. **"The Making of a Mexican American Dream."** *Pacific Standard.* March 6, 2017. http://psmag.com/magazine/the-making-of-a-mexi-can-american-dream.

Poole, Hilary W. *Immigrant Families.* Broomall, PA: Mason Crest, 2017.

Rosales, F. Arturo. *Chicano! The History of the Mexican American Civil Rights Movement.* Houston, TX: Arte Publico Press, 1996.

Websites

http://www.ocweekly.com/topic/ask-a-mexican-6568416
Author Gustavo Arellano answers reader questions about Mexican American culture, food, and politics.

http://www.proudtobemexican.com/home.html
Proud to Be Mexican (Orgulloso de ser Mexicano) collects news items about Mexican culture abroad and profiles successful Mexican Americans.

Series Glossary of Key Terms

acclimate to get used to something

assimilate become part of a different society, country, or group

bigotry treating the members of a racial or ethnic group with hatred and intolerance

culinary having to do with the preparing of food

diaspora a group of people who live outside the area in which they had lived for a long time or in which their ancestors lived

emigrate leave one's home country to live in another country

exodus a mass departure of people from one place to another

first-generation American someone born in the United States whose parents were foreign born

immigrants those who enter another country intending to stay permanently

naturalize to gain citizenship, with all its rights and privileges

oppression a system of forcing people to follow rules or a system that restricts freedoms

presentation in this series, the style in which food is plated and served

Index

Photo Credits

Author Bio

H.W. Poole is a writer and editor of books for young people, including the sets *Childhood Fears and Anxieties, Families Today, and Mental Illnesses and Disorders* (Mason Crest). She created the *Horrors of History* series (Charlesbridge) and the *Ecosystems* series (Facts On File). She was coauthor and editor of *The History of the Internet* (ABC-CLIO), which won the 2000 American Library Association RUSA award.